The Most Delicious Stir Fry Recipes

The Only Stir Fry Cookbook You Will Ever Need

TABLE OF CONTENTS

- SUGAR SNAP PEA PORK STIR FRY
- OKRA AND RICE STIR FRY
- MONGOLIAN VEGAN NOODLE STIR FRY
- LEFTOVER TURKEY STIR FRY
- KUNG PAO SHRIMP
- CAULIFLOWER RICE VEGGIE STIR FRY
- CHICKEN, MUSHROOM, AND GREEN BEAN STIR FRY
- TEMPEH STIR FRY IN A GINGERY PEANUT SAUCE
- SZECHUAN CHICKEN STIR FRY
- APPLE CIDER KALE STIR FRY
- CHILI SHRIMP NOODLE STIR FRY
- MANGO CHICKEN STIR FRY
- QUINOA AND BOK CHOY STIR FRY
- PORK AND HOLY BASIL STIR FRY
- COCONUT AND CASHEW CHICKEN STIR FRY
- BACON AND SAUSAGE CABBAGE STIR FRY
- BAMBOO SHOOT PORK STIR FRY
- STEAK AND SWEET POTATO NOODLE STIR FRY
- UDON NOODLE AND KIMCHI STIR FRY
- INDIAN CHICKEN STIR FRY

Shrimp, Leek and Watercress Stir-Fry

15 minutes. Serves 4.

- **2** small leeks
- **12** ounces large peeled and deveined shrimp
  Kosher salt and freshly ground black pepper
- **2** tablespoons extra-virgin olive oil
- **2** fresh long red mild chiles, such as finger or Fresno, thinly sliced at an angle
- **1** bunch watercress (7 ounces), tough stems and some leaves reserved for garnish

Lemon wedges, for serving

Stir Fry See mint

1 Trim any tough dark green tops off the leeks, keeping the tender green parts. If the leeks are thick, cut them lengthwise in half. Cut into 1-inch pieces crosswise, then wash well and dry well. Sprinkle the shrimp with salt and pepper.

2 Heat a large skillet or wok over high heat until a drop of water skitters across the surface. Add the oil and carefully swirl to coat; it should be shimmering. Add the leeks, sprinkle with salt, and cook, stirring occasionally, until browned in spots, 1 to 2 minutes. Add the chiles and cook, stirring, for 1 minute. Add the shrimp and cook, stirring occasionally, until it is lightly browned and opaque throughout, 3 to 4 minutes. Remove the skillet from the heat.

3 Fold in the watercress; it will wilt in the residual heat. Transfer to a serving plate and garnish with the watercress tops and flowers. Squeeze lemon juice on top and serve.

REN FULLER
For The Times
Prop styling by
NIDIA CUEVA

striding confidently to the rose garden on her sprawling, wildish ranch in Three River foothills of the Sierra Nevada. She has a long shovel in her hand, and there's this tension as learn. ¶ It isn't until her visitors exclaim about her abundant roses, the blooming tr Huston's commanding presence softens. ¶ "You really like them?" she asks anxiously 38-acre Flying Heart Ranch in the mid-1980s, the nicest description of it would have bee

STRUT LIKE A PEACOCK AROUND WILMINGTON
FOUR HOURS

SUNSET CRUISE WITH A BAND OF MISFITS
CHRIS ERSKINE

RELAXI TOGETE A SOUNI
MIND & B

Table of Contents

Conclusion

Introduction

Do you struggle to find the balance between the soy sauce, the rice vinegar, the honey, and the other ingredients you are stirring into your wok? If so, then buying this book will save you from your failed attempts to create that takeout stir fry that you like so much. This book will help you make it even better.

Offering you 40 different ways to prepare a stir fry, whether with meat or not, this is the only cookbook that will show you the true worth of your wok.

Delicious and nutritious, the stir fry recipes in this book will not only satisfy your tummy and taste buds, but they will also boost your immune and pack you with feel-good vibes.

Whether on rice or noodles, these amazing delicacies are simple to make, and they can all be mastered by you after the very first attempt.

Jump to the first recipe and see what I am talking about.

Sweet and Garlicky Chicken Stir Fry

Garlic, honey, carrots and broccoli accompany chicken in this delicious and simple-to-make stir fry that is cooked to perfection and fried in a savory sweet sauce that will have you licking your plate in no time.

Serves: 4

Ready In: 30 minutes

Ingredients:

- 2 cups Broccoli Florets
- 1 cup sliced Carrots
- ¼ cup Soy Sauce
- 3 tbsp. Honey
- 1 pound Chicken Breasts, cut into cubes
- ¼ cup Chicken Broth
- 2 tsp Cornstarch
- 4 Garlic Cloves, minced
- 2 tsp Cornstarch
- 1 tbsp. plus 1 tsp Oil
- ¼ tsp Salt
- ¼ tsp Pepper

Preparation:

Heat a teaspoon of oil in a pan over medium heat.

Add carrots and broccoli. Cook for about 3-4 minutes.

Transfer the veggies to a pan and heat the remaining oil in the pan.

Add chicken, salt, and pepper, and cook until golden.

Add garlic and cook for 30 more seconds.

Return the veggies to the pan.

In a bowl, whisk together the remaining ingredients.

Pour the sauce over and cook for a few minutes, until thickened.

Serve and enjoy!

Ramen Stir Fry

Packaged ramen noodles combined with a bunch of veggies in a sweet and flavorful sauce. This noodle dish is ready in only 20 minutes, and is the perfect choice for your Asian dinner nights.

Serves: 4

Ready In: 20 minutes

Ingredients:

- 9 ounces packaged Ramen Noodles
- 2 tbsp Sesame Oil
- 2 Chicken Flavor Packets
- 2 ½ cups chopped Veggies (asparagus, carrots, snow peas, celery, broccoli…)
- 1 cup chopped Onion
- 2 tbsp. Olive Oil
- 1/3 cup Hoisin Sauce
- 1 tbsp. granulated Garlic
- 1/3 cup Mr. Yoshida Sauce
- ¾ cup Cold Water

Preparation:

Bring a bowl of water to a boil and then cook the noodles in it for about 2 minutes, or until tender. Drain and set it aside.

In a skillet, heat the olive oil over medium heat.

Add onion and cook for 2 minutes.

Add the chopped vegetables and cook for 3 more minutes.

Stir in the ramen and remaining ingredients.

Toss to coat everything well.

Cook for 1 minute and serve immediately.

Enjoy!

Maple and Cashew Veggie Stir Fry

A sweet sauce with maple syrup, garlic, and ginger, combine the peppers, cauliflower, and broccoli in the most flavorful and delicious way. The cashew topping gives this stir fry a heavenly crunchiness and takes it to the next level.

Serves: 4

Ready In: 25 minutes

Ingredients:

- 1 tbsp. Olive Oil
- 1 ½ cups Cauliflower Florets
- 1 ½ cups Broccoli Florets
- ½ cup chopped Red Bell Pepper
- ½ cup Yellow Bell Pepper
- ½ cup Green Bell Pepper
- ½ tsp Salt
- ½ cup chopped Cashews
- 1 Green Onion, sliced

Sauce:

- 3 ½ tsp minced Garlic
- 1 ½ tbsp. Lemon Juice
- 1/3 cup Tamari Sauce
- 3 ½ tbsp. Maple Syrup
- 1 tsp toasted Sesame Oil
- 2 tsp minced Ginger
- 1 tsp Blackstrap Molasses
- 1 tbsp. Arrowroot Powder
- 1/3 cup Water

Preparation:

Heat the olive oil in a wok over the medium heat.

Add broccoli and peppers and cook for a couple of minutes, until soft.

Meanwhile, whisk together all of the sauce ingredients in a bowl.

Increase the heat to high and pour the sauce over the veggies.

Bring it to a slow boil, then reduce to simmer, and cook until thickened.

Stir in the cashews and green onions.

Serve immediately and enjoy!

Veggie Brown Rice Stir Fry

Who needs meat when there is this yummy recipe? Packed with brown rice, red cabbage, broccoli, zucchini, and bell pepper, this stir fry wrapped in irresistible garlicky flavor will blow your mind.

Serves: 4

Ready In: 45 minutes

Ingredients:

- ½ cup chopped Zucchini
- 1 cup chopped red Cabbage
- 1 Bell Pepper, chopped
- ½ Head of Broccoli, broken into Florets
- ½ cup uncooked Brown Rice
- 4 Garlic Cloves, minced
- 2 tbsp. Olive Oil
- Pinch of Cayenne Pepper
- 2 tbsp. Soy Sauce
- 1 tbsp. chopped Parsley

Preparation:

Cook the rice following the package instructions.

Add enough water in a wok to cover the veggies.

Bring it to a boil and then place the veggies in it.

Heat for 2 minutes, then drain and set aside.

Wipe the wok clean and heat the oil in it.

Add garlic, parsley, and cayenne, and cook for 1 minute, until fragrant.

Stir in the rice, veggies, and tamari. Cook for 2 minutes.

Serve immediately and enjoy!

Teriyaki Chicken Stir Fry

Teriyaki sauce is the star of this recipe and combined with the most famous Asian ingredients, it creates one marvelous dish that you will not be able to resist.

Serves: 4

Ready In: 30 minutes

Ingredients:

- 2 tbsp. Olive Oil
- 2 tbsp. Soy Sauce
- 2 pounds Frozen Veggie Mix
- 1 pound Chicken Breast, cut into chunks
- 2 tsp grated Ginger
- 2 tsp minced Garlic
- 1 tsp Rice Vinegar
- 1 tbsp. Cornstarch
- 1 tbsp. Water

Preparation:

In a wok, heat the oil over medium heat.

Add chicken and cook until golden brown on all sides.

Stir in the veggies and cook until soft.

In a bowl, whisk together the remaining ingredients.

Pour the sauce over the chicken and veggies and cook for 3 minutes, or until thickened.

Serve and enjoy!

Honey and Garlic Shrimp Stir Fry

Sweet and garlicky flavored, this stir fry with shrimp, white rice, and broccoli, is better than the Asian takeout you are used to. And the very first bite will convince you in that.

Serves: 4

Ready In: 30 minutes

Ingredients:

- 1 ½ cup cooked White Rice
- 1 ½ cups Broccoli Florets
- 1 pound Shrimp, peeled and deveined
- 1/3 cup Honey
- 1 tbsp. minced Garlic
- 1 tsp minced Ginger
- ¼ cup Soy Sauce
- 2 tsp Olive Oil
- Salt and Pepper, to taste

Preparation:

In a bowl, whisk together the ginger, garlic, soy sauce, and honey.

Place the shrimp and the broccoli in a Ziploc bag and pour half of the sauce over.

Seal and shake to coat well.

Let the mixture sit for 15 minutes.

Heat the olive oil in a pan and add the shrimp and broccoli along with the juices.

Cook for a minute or two, or until set.

Stir in the rice and pour the remaining marinade over.

Cook until cooked through.

Serve and enjoy!

Ground Turkey Stir Fry

This Thai-inspired ground turkey stir fry with peppers and basil in a sweet and tangy sauce is not only filling and delicious but it is also one of those meals that you simply devour.

Serves: 6

Ready In: 20 minutes

Ingredients:

- 1 Onion, chopped
- 1 ½ cups Basil Leaves
- 1 ½ pounds ground Turkey
- 1 Red Bell Pepper, cut into strips
- 1 tsp Avocado Oil
- 2 tsp minced Garlic

Sauce:

- 1 tbsp. Agave Nectar
- 1 tbsp. Fish Sauce
- 1 tbsp. Soy Sauce
- 2 tbsp. fresh Lime Juice
- 1 tbsp. Sriracha Sauce

Preparation:

Whisk together all of the sauce ingredients in a bowl. Set aside.

Heat the oil in a wok and cook the onion and peppers until soft.

Add garlic and cook for 30 seconds or so, or just until fragrant.

Add turkey and cook until it becomes browned.

Stir in the basil and cook until it becomes wilted.

Pour the sauce over and cook for 2 minutes.

Serve immediately and enjoy!

Mongolian Beef Stir Fry

Peppers, broccoli, water chestnut and flank steak star in this hoisin sauce delicacy that will water your mouth the seconds you start cooking. Rich and flavorful, this Mongolian stir fry satisfies all tastes.

Serves: 4

Ready In: 30 minutes

Ingredients:

- 1 pound Flank Steak, cut into strips
- 2 tbsp. Oil
- 3 tbsp. Cornstarch
- 1 cup chopped Peppers
- ½ cup sliced Water Chestnuts
- 3 Green Onions, chopped
- 1 Broccoli Head, cut into florets

Sauce:

- 2 tbsp. Rice Vinegar
- 1/3 cup Hoisin Sauce
- 2 tsp minced Garlic
- ½ tsp grated Ginger
- 1/3 cup Soy Sauce
- 2 tbsp. Brown Sugar
- ½ cup Water
- ½ tsp Chili Paste

Preparation:

Toss the beef with cornstarch and heat the oil in a pan over medium heat.

Add beef and cook until browned on all sides. Transfer to a plate.

Add the veggies and cook until soft, for a couple of minutes.

Meanwhile, whisk the sauce ingredients together in a bowl.

Pour the sauce over the veggies and add the beef to the pan.

Stir to combine and cook for a few minutes, or until the sauce thickens.

Serve and enjoy!

Simple Beef and Broccoli Stir Fry

If you are looking for a simple stir fry recipe with beef, then this is probably the most basic way to prepare it. Beef and broccoli in a simple sweet sauce with brown sugar and soy sauce.

Serves: 4

Ready In: 25 minutes

Ingredients:

- 1 pound Round Steak
- 2 tbsp. Vegetable Oil
- 4 cups Broccoli Florets
- ½ cup plus 2 tbsp. Water
- 3 tbsp. Cornstarch
- 1 Onion, sliced
- 2 tbsp. Brown Sugar
- 1 tsp ground Ginger
- 1/3 cup Soy Sauce
- ½ tsp Garlic Powder

Preparation:

Whisk together 2 tbsp. water, 2 tbsp. cornstarch, and the garlic powder, in a bowl.

Add the beef and toss to coat it well.

Heat half of the oil in a wok over the medium heat.

Add beef and cook until browned on all sides. Transfer to a plate.

Heat the remaining oil and cook the onion and broccoli until soft.

Return the beef to the pan.

In a bowl, whisk together the remaining ingredients.

Pour the sauce over the beef and veggies.

Cook for 2 more minutes, or until thickened.

Serve and enjoy!

Chicken Lo Mein

Chicken lo Mein is one of the most famous stir fry recipes, and if you are a fan of the Asian takeout meals, then this recipe is just what you need to make for dinner to satisfy your taste buds.

Serves: 6

Ready In: 30 minutes

Ingredients:

- 2 Chicken Breasts, cut into chunks
- 4 tbsp. Olive Oil
- 1 cup Chinese Cabbage, shredded
- 2 tbsp. Soy Sauce
- 2 cups sliced Shitake Mushrooms
- 1 Onion, chopped
- 1 cup grated Carrots
- 2 tap minced Garlic
- 1 tsp minced Ginger
- 16 ounces Ramen Noodles
- 2 Spring Onions, chopped

Sauce:

- 1 tbsp. Oyster Sauce
- 1 tsp Hoisin Sauce
- 1 tbsp. Brown Sugar
- 2 tbsp. Soy Sauce
- 1 tsp Pepper
- 2 tbsp. Dark Soy Sauce
- 1 tsp Sesame Oil

Preparation:

Cook the noodles according the package instructions. Drain and place in a bowl.

Toss the chicken with ginger, 2 tbsp. soy sauce, and ginger.

Use a wok to heat half of the olive oil and add the chicken.

Cook until golden on all sides, for about 5 minutes. Transfer to a plate.

Heat the rest oil in the wok.

Add the veggies, except the green onions, and cook for a few more minutes, until soft.

Move the chicken back to the wok.

Meanwhile, whisk together the sauce ingredients in a bowl. Pour the mixture over the chicken and veggies.

Stir to combine and cook for 2 minutes.

Serve over noodles and sprinkle with green onions.

Serve and enjoy!

Pepper Steak Stir Fry

Peppers, steak, green onions, ginger, and soy sauce are the main ingredients in this Chinese stir fry that is excellent served on rice. A colorful dish that is packed with rich flavors.

Serves: 4

Ready In: 30 minutes

Ingredients:

- 1 pound Sirloin Steak, cut into strips
- 1 ½ Bell Peppers (different colors), sliced
- 2 Green Onions, sliced
- 2 tbsp. minced Ginger
- 1 ½ tsp minced Garlic
- 2 tbsp. Olive Oil

Marinade:

- ¼ cup Soy Sauce
- 1 tbsp. Cornstarch
- 1/3 cup Water
- Pinch of Pepper
- 2 tbsp. Rice Wine Vinegar

Preparation:

Whisk the marinade ingredients in a bowl.

Place the steak in a Ziploc bag and pour the marinade over.

Seal the bag and shake to coat well. Let it marinate for 15 minutes.

Heat half of the oil in a wok.

Add the white parts of the peppers and onions, and cook until softened.

Add ginger and garlic and cook for an additional minute. Transfer to a plate.

Heat the remaining oil and add the steak, without the marinade.

Cook until the steak is browned on all sides.

Return the veggies to the wok along with the green parts of the onions.

Pour the marinade over and cook for 2 more minutes.

Serve and enjoy!

Thai Noodle Stir Fry

Originally called Pad See Ew, this popular Thai street food is consisting of stir fried noodles in a salty and sour, but very balanced sauce. Combined with chicken and Chinese broccoli, this is super enjoyable.

Serves: 4

Ready In: 30 minutes

Ingredients:

- 6 ounces Wide Rice Noodles
- 2 tbsp. Peanut Oil
- 2 Garlic Cloves, minced
- 1 cup chopped Chicken Thighs
- 1 Egg
- 4 cups Chinese Broccoli, leaves separated and chopped

Sauce:

- 2 tbsp. Dark Soy Sauce
- 2 tsp White Vinegar
- 2 tbsp Oyster Sauce
- 2 tbsp Water
- 2 tsp Sugar
- 2 tsp Regular Soy Sauce

Preparation:

Cook the noodles as stated on the package. Drain and place in a bowl.

Heat the oil in a wok and add garlic.

Cook for 1 minute until fragrant.

Add chicken and the stems of the Chinese Broccoli.

Cook until the chicken turns golden on all sides.

Move them to the side of the pan and add the egg.

Scramble and cook until set.

Add the noodles and the leaves of the broccoli.

Whisk all of the sauce ingredients in a bowl and pour the sauce over.

Cook until the leaves become wilted.

Serve immediately and enjoy!

Egg Roll Stir Fry

If you love eating egg rolls, then you will definitely fall in love with this recipe. Your favorite egg roll filling as a full stir fry meal. Serve over rice if you want to.

Serves: 4

Ready In: 20 minutes

Ingredients:

- 1 pound ground Pork
- 1 Onion, diced
- 1 tbsp. Oil
- 1 small Cabbage Head, sliced
- 3 Carrots, sliced
- 2 tbsp. Sesame Oil
- 4 Garlic Cloves, minced
- ¼ cup Soy Sauce
- ½ tsp Pepper
- 1 tbsp. grated Ginger

Preparation:

Heat the oil in a pan over medium heat.

Cook the onions and pork until the pork becomes browned.

Add the carrots and cabbage and cook for 3 more minutes.

Meanwhile whisk together the ginger, soy sauce, garlic, pepper, and sesame oil, in a bowl.

Pour the mixture over.

Cook for a few more minutes.

Serve and enjoy!

Sriracha Beef and Cabbage Stir Fry

Spiced up with some sriracha and wrapped up beautifully in a sweet and salty sauce, this stir fry with beef and cabbage has just what you are looking for in Asian takeout meals.

Serves: 4

Ready In: 30 minutes

Ingredients:

- ½ Green Cabbage, thinly sliced
- 2 Carrots, shredded
- 3 Green Onions, chopped

- ½ pound ground Beef
- 1 tbsp. grated Ginger
- 1 tbsp. toasted Sesame Oil
- 2 tbsp. Soy Sauce
- 2 tbsp. Sriracha
- ½ tbsp. Olive Oil
- 1 tsp minced Garlic
- ½ tbsp. Brown Sugar

Preparation:

In a bowl, whisk together the soy sauce, brown sugar, half of sriracha, and sesame oil. Set aside.

Heat the oil in a wok and add the beef, ginger, and garlic.

Cook until the beef is browned.

Add the veggies and cook for a few more minutes, until the cabbage reaches your desired consistency.

Pour the sauce over and cook for a few more minutes.

Serve drizzled with the remaining Sriracha.

Enjoy!

Lemon Chicken Stir Fry

Packed with veggies, rich in amazing flavors, and most importantly, healthy, this lemon chicken stir fry is just what you need to boost your immune during those cold winter days. Serve over brown rice for a full meal.

Serves: 4

Ready In: 22 minutes

Ingredients:

- 1 pound Chicken Breasts, cut into strips
- ½ Onion, chopped
- 1 pound Zucchini, chopped
- 6 ounces Mushrooms, sliced
- 2 tsp Sesame Oil

Sauce:

- 1 cup Chicken Broth
- ½ tbsp. Sesame Oil
- 1 tbsp. Lemon Juice
- Zest of ½ Lemon
- ½ tbsp. Sesame Oil
- ½ tsp Fish Sauce
- 1 tbsp. Soy Sauce
- 2 Garlic Cloves, minced
- 1 ½ tbsp. Cornstarch

Preparation:

Whisk together all of the sauce ingredients in a bowl. Set it aside.

Heat a wok over high heat and add half of the oil.

Cook the chicken for 5 minutes, or until it is golden on all sides. Then transfer to a plate.

Heat the remaining oil and add the veggies.

Cook until they become soft.

Return the chicken to the pan and pour the sauce over.

Cook for a few minutes. Serve and enjoy!

Veggie Tofu Stir Fry

Peppers and broccoli with tofu in a red curry sauce is all you need for dinner. Unique in flavor and fragrant and rich in the most amazing taste, this stir fry will be the favorite one for every vegetarian.

Serves: 4

Ready In: 20 minutes

Ingredients:

- 1 pound Tofu, cubed
- 1 Red Bell Pepper, sliced
- 1 Yellow Bell Pepper, sliced
- 1 Green Bell Pepper, sliced
- 1 tbsp. grated Ginger
- 12 ounces Broccoli Florets
- 3 tbsp. Sesame Oil
- 3 tbsp. Water
- 1 ½ tsp Arrowroot
- 2 tbsp Red Curry Paste
- 1/3 cup Soy Sauce

Preparation:

In a bowl, whisk together the water, arrowroot, soy sauce, and red curry paste. Set aside.

Heat the sesame oil in a wok over the medium heat.

Add tofu and cook for about 3 minutes.

Then stir in the peppers and ginger and cook until soft, about 5 minutes.

Add broccoli florets and cook for 2 minutes.

Pour the sauce over and cook until it thickens, a couple of minutes.

Serve and enjoy!

Shrimp and Zoodle Stir Fry

Shrimp, zoodles, snap peas, carrots, bell pepper, and onions give this stir fry a delectable and unique flavor that it's easy to resist. Serve this recipe as it is and enjoy.

Serves: 4

Ready In: 25 minutes

Ingredients:

- 1 pound Shrimp, peeled and deveined
- 2/3 cup sliced Red Onions
- 1 cup Snap Peas
- 2 Zucchinis, spiralized into noodles
- 2 tsp Cornstarch
- 1 Bell Pepper, sliced
- ½ cup shredded Carrots
- 1 tsp minced Ginger
- ½ cup Chicken Broth
- 1 tbsp. Soy Sauce
- ¼ cup Hoisin Sauce
- 1 tbsp. minced Garlic
- 3 tbsp. Olive Oil

Preparation:

Whisk the cornstarch, hoisin sauce, soy sauce, and broth, in a bowl. Set aside.

Heat 2 tbsp. of the oil in a wok over the medium heat.

Add garlic and ginger and cook for 1 minute.

Add shrimp and cook on all sides, for about 3 minutes in total. Transfer to a bowl.

Heat the remaining oil and add onions and peppers.

Cook until soft and stir in the carrots and snap peas. Cook for additional 3 minutes.

Pour the sauce over and cook for a couple of minutes, or until thickened.

Stir in the shrimp and noodles, and cook for 1 minute.

Serve and enjoy!

Zucchini, Squash, and Chicken in a Sweet Chili Sauce

A sweet and chili stir fry with chicken, squash, and zucchini. The rice wine vinegar makes all the difference so be sure not to leave it out or substitute with another ingredient.

Serves: 6

Ready In: 30 minutes

Ingredients:

- 4 tbsp. Olive Oil
- 2 small Zucchini, chopped
- 2 small Squashes, chopped
- 3 Chicken Breasts, chopped
- 1 Onion, chopped
- Salt and Pepper, to taste

Sauce:

- 1 tbsp. Cold Water
- ¾ cup Sweet and Chili Sauce
- 2 tbsp. Honey
- 3 tbsp Soy Sauce
- 1 tbsp. Cornstarch
- 1 tbsp. Rice Wine Vinegar

Preparation:

Heat half of the oil in a wok on the medium heat.

Add chicken, season with some pepper and salt, and cook until golden on all sides. Transfer to a plate.

Heat the remaining oil and sauté the onions for 2 minutes.

Add squash and zucchini and cook for few more minutes until tender, but not soggy.

Meanwhile, whisk together the sauce ingredients, in a bowl.

Pour over the vegggies and stir in the chicken.

Cook until the sauce thickens and serve.

Rainbow Veggie Stir Fry

Different veggie colors = different vitamins. And this stir fry is packed with them all. Prepare with your favorite sauce and serve over rice or noodles. Absolutely yummy!

Serves: 2

Ready In: 20 minutes

Ingredients:

- ¼ Red Cabbage, chopped
- 1 Large Red Bell Pepper, chopped

- ½ Broccoli Head, broken into florets
- 2 Carrots, shredded
- ½ Yellow Bell Pepper, chopped
- 1 tbsp. Lime Juice
- 2 tbsp. Oil
- 1 cup favorite Sauce (I suggest Asian Peanut Sauce)

Preparation:

Heat half of the oil in a medium heat in a wok.

Add onion and garlic and cook for 1 minute.

Add peppers and continue cooking for another 3 minutes.

Add the remaining oil and stir in the rest of the ingredients.

Cook until the veggies are tender.

Pour the sauce over and cook for 2 more minutes.

Serve over rice and noodles.

Enjoy!

Sugar Snap Pea Pork Stir Fry

This stir fry with pork loin, sugar snap peas, carrots, peppers, and rice, is a real crowd pleaser. Prepared in a simple sweet and tangy sauce, this stir fry is the ultimate Chinese dinner.

Serves: 4

Ready In: 30 minutes

Ingredients:

- 1 pound Boneless Pork Loin, chopped
- 1 tbsp. Cornstarch
- 1 tbsp. Oyster Sauce

- 3 tbsp. Soy Sauce
- 1 tbsp. Lime Juice
- 3 tbsp. Canola Oil
- 1 tbsp. minced Ginger
- 3 Scallions, chopped
- 2 Carrots, sliced
- 1 tbsp. chopped Cilantro
- 2 tsp minced Garlic
- 1 Red Bell Pepper, cut into strips
- 8 ounces Sugar Snap Peas
- 2 cups cooked White Rice

Preparation:

Place the pork, cornstarch and 1 tbsp. soy sauce, in a bowl. Mix to coat well.

In another bowl, whisk together the rest of the soy sauce, lime juice, and oyster sauce, and set aside.

Heat 2 tbsp. of oil in wok and add the pork.

Cook until the pork is browned on all sides. Transfer to a plate.

Heat the remaining oil and add the other fragrant ingredients (ginger, scallion, garlic). Cook for only one minute.

Add carrots and peppers and cook for 2 more minutes.

Stir in the sugar snap peas and cook for additional 2-3 minutes.

Add the pork and pour the sauce over.

Stir in the rice.

Cook for a minute or two more until cooked through and combined.

Serve immediately and enjoy!

Okra and Rice Stir Fry

Made with only ingredients and ready in just 10 minutes, this stir fry with okra and cooked rice is the definition of a quick and easy dinner.

Serves: 2

Ready In: 10 minutes

Ingredients:

- 2 dried Chili Peppers
- 1 ½ cups cooked White Rice
- 7 ounces Okra, chopped
- 2 tbsp. Soy Sauce
- 1 tsp Sichuan Peppercorn

Preparation:

Grease your wok well with cooking spray and heat over medium heat.

Add the Sichuan peppercorn and cook for a minute, until it becomes dark and fragrant.

Break the chili peppers into the wok.

Add the okra and cook for 1 minute.

Add half of soy sauce and cook the mixture for 3 minutes.

Stir in the cooked rice and the remaining soy sauce and cook for another minute or so.

Serve and enjoy!

Mongolian Vegan Noodle Stir Fry

If you are a vegan and a busy worker, you will highly appreciate this quick and easy dish. Made with purple cabbage, kale, bell pepper and baby corn, this nutrient-pack stir fry is a good immune booster.

Serves: 6

Ready In: 15 minutes

Ingredients:

- 9 Noodles of Choice
- 1 cup shredded Purple Cabbage
- 1 Bell Pepper, sliced
- 2 cups chopped Kale
- ½ cup Baby Corn
- 2 tbsp. Sugar
- 3 tsp Red Chilly Sauce
- 1 tbsp. plus 2 tsp Oil
- 3 tbsp. plus 1 tsp Dark Soy Sauce
- 2 tbsp. grated Ginger
- 1 tbsp. Sesame Oil
- 1 tsp Pepper

Preparation:

Cook the noodles following the package instructions.

Drain and toss with 1 tsp soy sauce, 2 tsp oil, and 1 tsp chili sauce. Set aside.

In a bowl, whisk together the seasonings, sauces, and sugar.

Heat the oil in a wok over the medium heat.

Add ginger and cook for 30-35 seconds.

Add the vegies and cook until they are tender.

Stir in the noodles and pour the sauce over.

Cook for about 2 minutes, or until well combined and cooked through.

Serve immediately and enjoy!

Leftover Turkey Stir Fry

When you don't know what to do with your leftover turkey, here is a solution – make this delightful stir fry. Ready in just 20 minutes. This veggie and turkey stir fry in a fragrant sauce will please everyone.

Serves: 4

Ready In: 20 minutes

Ingredients:

- 1 pound leftover Turkey Meat, shredded
- 1 pound frozen Veggie Mix (broccoli, carrots, peas, etc.)
- 1 tbsp. Rice Vinegar
- 1 Onion, chopped
- 1 tbsp. minced Ginger
- 1 tbsp. minced Garlic
- 2 tsp Sesame Oil
- 3 tbsp. Soy Sauce
- 1 tbsp. Honey
- 1 tsp Cornstarch
- 2 tbsp. Avocado Oil

Preparation:

Place the veggies in a microwave safe bowl and add a splash of water.

Microwave for 3-4 minutes, or until tender.

In a bowl, whisk together the honey, rice vinegar, soy sauce, and cornstarch. Set aside.

Heat the avocado oil in a wok over the medium heat.

Add onions and cook for 3 minutes, or as long as it needs for them to become soft.

Add the garlic and then stir the ginger into the well as well. Cook for 30 seconds.

Stir in the veggies and turkey.

Pour the sauce over and cook until it thickens, 2-3 minutes.

Serve and enjoy!

Kung Pao Shrimp

Shrimp, veggies, and peanuts are the stars of this classic Asian dish. If you love this spicy and sweet take out, then you will be amazed to know that you can easily make one in your own kitchen.

Serves: 4

Ready In: 20 minutes

Ingredients:

- ½ Red Bell Pepper, cut into strips
- ½ Green Bell Pepper, cut into strips
- 1 pound large Shrimp, peeled and deveined
- 1 tbsp. Oil
- ½ Yellow Onion, chopped
- 1 tsp minced Garlic
- 4 dried Red Chilies, seeded and halved
- ½ cup unsalted Peanuts

Sauce:

- 2 tsp Cornstarch
- 1 tbsp. Hoisin Sauce
- 2 tsp Sugar
- 2 tbsp. Water
- 2 tbsp. Soy Sauce
- 2 tsp Sesame Oil

Preparation:

Heat the oil in wok over the medium heat.

Add onion and cook for 3 minutes.

Add the peppers and cook for additional 2-3 minutes.

Stir in the garlic and cook only for 30 seconds.

Add shrimp and cook on all sides for about 3 minutes in total.

Meanwhile, whisk together all of the sauce ingredients in a bowl.

Pour the sauce over.

Cook until it thickens, about 2-3 minutes.

Serve immediately and enjoy!

Cauliflower Rice Veggie Stir Fry

Light and packed with veggies, this nutritious stir fry in a finger-licking sweet, tangy, and gingery sauce will be your new favorite dish. Throw in some marinated tofu for extra protein if you want to.

Serves: 4

Ready In: 40 minutes

Ingredients:

- 4 cups Cauliflower Rice (ground in a food processor)
- ½ cup Peas
- 1 cup grated Carrots
- 1 Onion, chopped
- 3 Garlic Cloves, minced
- 1 cup Broccoli Florets
- ¼ cup Soy Sauce
- 1 ½ tbsp. Honey
- 1 tsp Red Pepper Flakes
- 1/2 tsp Ginger Powder
- ¼ cup Water

Preparation:

Whisk together all of the ingredients except the veggies, in a bowl.

Grease a wok with cooking spray.

Add the onion and cook for a few minutes or until soft.

Add the remaining veggies, except the cauliflower rice, and cook for 5 minutes.

Stir in the rice and cook for additional 5 minutes.

Pour the sauce over and cook until thickened.

Serve and enjoy!

Chicken, Mushroom, and Green Bean Stir Fry

Cremini mushrooms and green beans accompany chicken for this lovely stir fry rich in delightful garlicky and gingery sauce. Serve over white rice an enjoy.

Serves: 4

Ready In: 30 minutes

Ingredients:

- 1 pound Chicken Breasts, chopped
- 30 French Green Beans, halved
- 2 tbsp. Canola Oil
- ¼ cup Cornstarch
- 1 tbsp. Sesame Oil
- 2 tsp minced Ginger
- 1 tsp minced Garlic
- ¼ cup Cornstarch
- ¼ cup Soy Sauce

Preparation:

Heat the sesame oil and canola oil in a wok over the medium heat.

Add chicken and cook until it becomes golden on all sides. Transfer to a plate.

Add the mushrooms and cook for 3 minutes.

Stir in green beans and cook for 3 minutes.

Stir in garlic and ginger and cook for additional 30 seconds.

Return the chicken and pour the sauce over.

Cook for 2 more minutes.

Serve and enjoy!

Tempeh Stir Fry in a Gingery Peanut Sauce

Rich and creamy in texture thanks to the peanut butter, this vegan stir fry with marinated tempeh and a bunch of veggies is served over white rice for a filling and delicious dinner.

Serves: 4

Ready In: 50 minutes

Ingredients:

- 1 cup shredded Carrots
- 1 cup chopped Kale
- 1 cup shredded Red Cabbage
- 2 cups White Rice

Tempeh:

- 8 ounces Organic Tempeh
- ¼ cup Water
- 1 tsp grated Ginger
- ¼ cup Soy Sauce
- 1 Garlic Clove, minced

Sauce:

- ¾ cup Peanut Butter
- 1 Garlic Clove, minced
- ¼ cup Water
- ¼ cup Soy Sauce
- 1 tsp grated Ginger
- 1 tbsp. Sesame Oil

Preparation:

Chop the tempeh and place in the microwave for a few minutes.

Place in a bowl and stir in the marinade ingredients. Let marinate for 30 minutes.

Preheat the oven for 350 degrees F.

Arrange the tempeh chunks on a lined baking sheet and bake for 15 minutes, turning once.

Meanwhile, cook the rice according the package instructions.

Whisk together all of the ingredients for the sauce.

Grease a wok with cooking spray and cook the veggies for a few minutes, until soft.

Add the tempeh and pour the sauce over.

Cook for a few minutes, or until thickened.

Serve and enjoy!

Szechuan Chicken Stir Fry

Chili paste and a bunch of colorful vegetables give this Szechuan chicken stir fry a delicious and spicy taste. Easy to make, delightful, and super nutritious, this recipe is a real keeper.

Serves: 4

Ready In: 25 minutes

Ingredients:

- 1 Egg, whisked
- 1 Onion, julienned
- ½ pound Chicken Breasts, chopped
- 2 tsp minced Garlic
- ½ Red Bell Pepper, chopped
- 1 tsp grated Ginger
- 2 tbsp. Vegetable Oil
- 2 tsp Cornstarch
- 5 Shitake Mushrooms, sliced
- ½ Green Bell Pepper, chopped

Sauce:

- ¼ cup Chicken Stock
- 1 tbsp. Spicy Chili Crisp
- 1 tbsp. Chile Paste
- 1 tsp Cornstarch
- 1 ½ tbsp. Soy Sauce
- ½ tbsp. Rice Vinegar

Preparation:

Combine the chicken, egg, and cornstarch in a bowl and let marinate for 5 minutes.

In another bowl, whisk together all of the remaining ingredients.

Heat half of the oil in a pan and add chicken.

Cook until it becomes golden on all sides. Transfer to a plate.

Heat the remaining oil and add the veggies.

Cook for a few minutes, until soft.

Add chicken and pour the sauce over.

Cook for a few more minutes, until everything is well coated and the sauce is thickened.

Serve and enjoy!

Apple Cider Kale Stir Fry

Kale, veggies, and apple combined in a delicious apple cider sauce and stir fried to perfection, make one super satisfying entrée. Sparkling wine is probably the best accompaniment.

Serves: 4

Ready In: 40 minutes

Ingredients:

- 1 Bunch of Kale, chopped
- ¼ Cabbage, sliced
- 1 Green Apple, sliced

- 2 Carrots, spiralized or grated

- 1 Onion, minced

- 1 Green Apple, thinly sliced

- 1 tbsp. Olive Oil

- ½ block Extra Firm Tofu, cubed

Sauce:

- 2 tbsp. Spy Sauce

- 1 cup Apple Cider

- 1 tbsp Apple Cider Vinegar

Preparation:

First, make the sauce. Pour the apple cider in a saucepan over medium heat and let simmer for 20 minutes or so, until it is reduced to about a quarter of a cup.

Stir in the vinegar and soy sauce.

Add the tofu and marinate until ready to cook.

Heat the oil in a pan over medium heat.

Add the minced onion and cook for 2 minutes.

Add cabbage and cook for 3 minutes.

Stir in the kale and carrots.

Cover the pan and cook until the kale is wilted.

Add tofu along with the marinade.

Stir in the apples and serve.

Enjoy!

Chili Shrimp Noodle Stir Fry

If you have ever been to Bangkok then you know how absolutely amazing their street food is. This recipe taste just like that. A noodle and shrimp stir fry that will blow your mind.

Serves: 4

Ready In: 15 minutes

Ingredients:

- 1 tbsp. Canola Oil
- 16 Shrimp, peeled and deveined
- 2 Thai Chilies
- 2 tbsp Fish Sauce
- 2 tbsp Dark Soy Sauce
- 1 Egg, whisked
- 1 Tomato, chopped
- 2 tsp chopped Kaffir Lime Leaves
- 2 tsp minced Garlic
- 8 ounces dried Rice Noodles

Preparation:

Cook the noodles according to the package instructions. Drain and set aside.

Heat the oil in a wok and add garlic. Cook for 30 seconds.

Add shrimp and cook until they become opaque. About 3 minutes.

Add the egg and stir in a couple of seconds until set.

Stir in the remaining ingredients and cook until the sauce becomes bubbling.

Add the rice noodles and stir to coat well.

Serve immediately.

Enjoy!

Mango Chicken Stir Fry

Chicken, bell pepper, and mango in a sweet and slightly chili mango sauce for the most incredible dinner ever. Serve over brown rice for a full meal. You can add some ginger for another fragrant hint.

Serves: 4

Ready In: 30 minutes

Ingredients:

- 3 Chicken Breasts, chopped
- 1 Red Bell Pepper, chopped
- 1 Mango, peeled and sliced
- 1 tsp minced Garlic
- 1 tsp White Vinegar
- ½ tsp Chili Flakes
- 1 ¼ cups Mango Chutney

Preparation:

Spray a pan with cooking spray and heat it over medium heat.

Add chicken and cook until it is golden on all sides.

Add peppers and cook for 3 minutes, or until soft.

Stir in the remaining ingredients, except the mango, and cook until the sauce begins to bubble.

Add the mango slices at this point.

Serve over rice.

Enjoy!

Quinoa and Bok Choy Stir Fry

Sweet and tangy at the same time, this stir fried made with quinoa, bok choy, peppers, mushrooms, and asparagus is the perfect vegetarian dinner. If you are a meat lover, know that some ground meat can be the perfect addition to this recipe.

Serves: 2

Ready In: 20 minutes

Ingredients:

- 1 cup sliced Mushrooms
- 5 Asparagus Spears, chopped
- ½ cup cooked Quinoa
- 1 tbsp Vegetable Oil
- 1 cup sliced Bell Pepppers
- 1 Head Bok Choy, sliced
- 1 ½ tsp minced Ginger
- 2 tbsp. toasted Sesame Seeds

Sauce:

- ½ tbsp. Lime Juice
- 5 tbsp. Soy Sauce
- 1 ¾ tsp Cornstarch
- ½ tbsp Sesame Oil
- 1 ½ tsp Honey

Preparation:

Heat the oil in a wok over the medium heat.

Add the peppers, asparagus, mushrooms, bok choy, and ginger.

Cook for about 5 minutes.

Meanwhile, whisk together the sauce ingredients, in a bowl.

Pour the sauce over the veggies.

Stir and cook until thickened.

Stir in quinoa and sesame seeds before serving. Enjoy!

Pork and Holy Basil Stir Fry

The holy basil in this recipe gives the pork a very unique almost licorice-like taste that is very addictive. The Holland chilies wrap this up beautifully. A definite must try!

Serves: 4

Ready In: 30 minutes

Ingredients:

- 2 Shallots, chopped
- 1 tsp Sugar
- 1 pound ground Pork
- 1/3 cup Chicken Broth

- 1 tbsp. Soy Sauce
- 7 Garlic Cloves, minced
- 3 Holland Chilies, thinly sliced
- 1 tbsp. Fish Sauce
- 2 tsp Oyster Sauce
- 1 ½ cups Holy Basil

Preparation:

Heat the oil in a wok over the medium heat.

Add shallots and garlic. Cook for about 3 minutes.

Stir the chilies in and cook for one more minute.

Add pork and cook until browned.

Stir in the sugar and sauces and cook for 2 more minutes.

Add the holy basil and cook until wilted.

Serve on rice.

Enjoy!

Coconut and Cashew Chicken Stir Fry

Light stir fry with chicken, peas in a coconut and honey sauce with a crunchy cashew topping. Does it get better than that? Serve over cooked white rice, sprinkle with extra chopped green onions, and enjoy.

Serves: 4

Ready In: 30 minutes

Ingredients:

- 1 pound Chicken Breast, chopped
- 2 tsp minced Garlic
- 1 cup Snow Peas
- ½ Onion, chopped
- 1 Red Bell Pepper, chopped
- 1 tsp grated Ginger
- ½ cup Cornstarch
- ¼ tsp Garlic Powder
- ¼ tsp Ginger Powder
- ½ tsp Salt
- ¼ cup Coconut Flakes
- 1 cup Cashews

Sauce:

- ½ cup Honey
- 3 tbsp. Apple Cider Vinegar
- 2 tsp Sriracha
- ½ cup Coconut Milk
- 2 tsp Cornstarch
- 2 tbsp Soy Sauce
- Salt and Pepper, to taste

Preparation:

Whisk together the sauce ingredients and set the mixture aside.

Coat the chicken with ginger powder, garlic powder, cornstarch and salt.

Grease a wok with some cooking spray and cook the chicken until golden; Transfer to a plate.

Add onions and pepper and cook for 3 minutes.

Add snow peas and chicken to the pan.

Pour the sauce over.

Cook for a few minutes, or until thickened.

Serve topped with coconut flakes and cashews.

Enjoy!

Bacon and Sausage Cabbage Stir Fry

Who says that stir fry has to be Asian? Try this sausage and bacon stir fry with cabbage and peppers, and see what I am talking about. Meaty and rich in flavors, this recipe surely satisfies.

Serves: 4

Ready In: 30 minutes

Ingredients:

- 1 ½ tbsp. Canola Oil
- 4 slices Bacon
- 1 Onion, chopped
- 1 pound Kielbasa Sausage, sliced
- 2 tsp minced Garlic
- 1 Red Bell Pepper, sliced
- 1 Cabbage Head, sliced
- Salt and Pepper, to taste

Preparation:

Cook the bacon in a wok over high heat, until crispy. Transfer to a plate.

Add ½ tbsp. oil and kielbasa and cook it until it becomes browned on all sides. Transfer the kielbasa to the plate.

Add the remaining oil and onion and peppers.

Cook until the veggies become soft, about 3 minutes.

Add garlic and cook for another minute.

Stir in the cabbage and cook for 3 minutes.

Add kielbasa and crumble the bacon over.

Season with salt and pepper and serve.

Enjoy!

Bamboo Shoot Pork Stir Fry

Bamboo shoots in a stir fry? Now that is what I call the ultimate Asian dish. So, easy and simple to make, and yet so rich in flavor, this dish will keep your family coming back for more.

Serves: 4

Ready In: 30 minutes

Ingredients:

- 3 Thai Chili Peppers, chopped
- 1 cup Jasmine Rice

- 2 Green Onions, chopped
- 2 cups Bamboo Shoots, cut into strips
- 3 Kaffir Lime Leaves, sliced
- 1 cup ground Pork
- 1 tbsp Oyster Sauce
- 2 tbsp. Thin Soy Sauce
- 3 Garlic Cloves, minced

Preparation:

Cook the rice following the package instructions.

Grease a wok with cooking spray over medium heat.

Add chilies and garlic and cook for about a minute.

Add the pork and cook it until it becomes browned.

Stir in the bamboo shoots and the oyster sauce.

After a minute, add the lime leaves and onions and cook for 2 more minutes.

Stir in the soy sauce and the cooked rice.

Serve and enjoy!

Steak and Sweet Potato Noodle Stir Fry

Steak and sweet potato noodles in a soy sauce and gingery sauce and with sesame seeds. This recipe is the best definition of an Asian Stir Fry.

Serves: 2

Ready In: 30 minutes

Ingredients:

- 1 cup Sweet Potato Noodles
- ½ pound Flank Steak, cut into strips
- 1 Bell Pepper, cut into strips
- 2 tbsp. Olive Oil
- ¼ Onion, chopped
- 2 tsp Garlic, minced
- 1/3 cup Soy Sauce
- 1 tbsp. Honey
- 1 tsp Sesame Oil
- ¼ cup Chicken Broth
- 1 tsp grated Ginger
- 1 tsp Vinegar
- 2 tbsp. Sesame Seeds

Preparation:

Heat half of the oil in a pan and add the sweet potato noodles.

Cook for a few minutes, on all sides. Transfer to a plate.

Heat the remaining oil and add the onion and peppers.

Cook for 2 minutes and add the garlic.

After 30 seconds, add the steak and cook until it becomes browned on all sides.

Add the sweet potato noodles and cook everything together for another minute.

Meanwhile, whisk together the honey, soy sauce, ginger, broth, and sesame oil.

Pour the sauce over and cook for a few minutes, until it thickens.

Serve topped with sesame seeds.

Enjoy!

Udon Noodle and Kimchi Stir Fry

Ready in just 15 minutes, this stir fry is the ultimate easy meal to prepare in a jiffy on those busy weeknights. Prepare in a spicy and super delicious Korean sauce, this stir fry is just addictive.

Serves: 2

Ready In: 15 minutes

Ingredients:

- 2 packs of Udon Noodles
- 1 cup Kimchi

- ¼ Onion, sliced
- 4 slices Bacon
- 1 Green Onion, sliced
- 1 tbsp. Olive Oil

Sauce:

- 1 tbsp. Korean Chili Flakes
- 1 tbsp. Honey
- 1 tbsp. Sugar
- ½ tbsp. Chili Paste
- ½ tsp minced Garlic
- 1 tbsp. Soy Sauce
- 1 tsp Rice Vinegar
- 1 tsp Sesame Oil

Preparation:

Cook the noodles following the package instructions, Drain and set them aside.

Heat the oil in a pan over medium heat.

Add onions and cook for 3 minutes.

Add bacon and cook until crispy.

Stir in kimchi and cook until wilted.

Meanwhile, whisk together the sauce ingredients in a bowl.

Pour over the kimchi mixture.

Stir in the noodles to coat well.

Serve immediately and enjoy!

Indian Chicken Stir Fry

Love Indian food? Then I really have nothing else to say except that you will go absolutely crazy about this recipe. Creamy, gingery, garlicky, this stir fry is the ultimate definition of comfort food.

Serves: 4

Ready In: 20 minutes

Ingredients:

- 1 Bell Pepper, diced
- 4 tbsp. Olive Oil

- 1 tbsp. Cream
- ½ cup Yogurt
- 2 Chicken Breasts, chopped
- 1 Onion, diced
- 1 tbsp. Tomato Paste
- 1 Green Chili, chopped
- 1 tsp minced Garlic
- 2 tsp grated Ginger
- 1 tsp Cumin Powder
- ½ tsp Turmeric Powder
- 1 tsp Coriander
- ¼ tsp Red Chili Flakes
- ¼ tsp Salt

Preparation:

Heat half of the oil in wok over the medium heat.

Add onions and pepper and cook for 2 minutes. Transfer to a plate.

Heat the remaining oil and add the chicken.

Cook until it is browned on all sides.

Stir in all of the spices (the last 5 ingredients), and cook for 2 more minutes.

Add the yogurt and cream.

Stir in the remaining ingredients, including the onions and peppers.

Cook for a few minutes.

Serve immediately and enjoy!

Tomato Beef Stir Fry

Tomatoes, beef, and a hot wok are the stars of this amazing stir fry that you will not be able to resist. Great served with noodles, but even more irresistible over white rice. Give it a try and see for yourself.

Serves: 4

Ready In: 80 minutes

Ingredients:

Beef:

- 1 pound Flank Steak
- 1 tbsp. Cornstarch
- 1 tsp Oil
- ¼ tsp Salt

Stir-Fry:

- 3 tbsp. Oil
- 1 tsp minced Garlic
- 1 tbsp. Shaoxing Wine
- ½ tbsp. Cornstarch whisked with 1 tbsp. Water
- 2 Ginger Slices
- ¼ cup sliced Shallots
- 5 Tomatoes, chopped

Sauce:

- 2 tbsp. Ketchup
- 2 tbsp Soy Sauce
- ½ tsp Sesame Oil
- 1 ½ tsp Sugar

Preparation:

Combine the beef ingredients in a bowl. Cover and let marinate for 1 hour.

Heat 1 tbsp oil in a hot wok and add the beef.

Cook until browned on all sides. Transfer to a plate.

Heat another tbsp of oil and add ginger.

Add shallots and garlic and cook for another minute.

Stir in the tomatoes and simmer for 2 minutes.

Stir in the wine and give it a stir.

Meanwhile whish together the sauce ingredients.

Pour the mixture over the sauce.

Stir in the beef.

Cook until the sauce is thickened.

Serve and enjoy!

Conclusion

See? I told you there were numerous ways in which you can prepare quick and easy and yet elegant and delectable stir fry. Now, all that you should do is heat your wok and start cooking.

Did you find these recipes tasty? Leave a review and let the others know. Your feedback will be greatly appreciated.

Thank you and happy stir frying!

Made in the USA
San Bernardino, CA
17 June 2019